# Stay Safe!
# On the road

Lisa Bruce

Heinemann
LIBRARY

Little Nippers

**www.heinemann.co.uk/library**
Visit our website to find out more information about **Heinemann Library** books.

To order:
☎ Phone 44 (0) 1865 888066
📄 Send a fax to 44 (0) 1865 314091
💻 Visit the Heinemann Bookshop at www.heinemann.co.uk/library to browse our catalogue and order online.

First published in Great Britain by Heinemann Library, Halley Court, Jordan Hill, Oxford OX2 8EJ, part of Harcourt Education.
Heinemann is a registered trademark of Harcourt Education Ltd.

© Harcourt Education Ltd 2003

Editorial: Jilly Attwood and Claire Throp
Design: Jo Hinton-Malivoire and bigtop, Bicester, UK
Models made by: Jo Brooker
Picture Research: Rosie Garai
Production: Séverine Ribierre

Originated by Dot Gradations
Printed and bound in China by South China Printing Company

ISBN 0 431 17271 4 (hardback)
07 06 05 04 03
10 9 8 7 6 5 4 3 2 1

ISBN 0 431 17276 5 (paperback)
07 06 05 04 03
10 9 8 7 6 5 4 3 2 1

**British Library Cataloguing in Publication Data**
Bruce, Lisa
Stay safe on the road – (Little Nippers)
363.1'257
A full catalogue record for this book is available from the British Library.

**Acknowledgements**
The publishers would like to thank the following for permission to reproduce photographs: Collections pp. **12**, **17** (Paul Bryans), **13** (Gordon Hill), 21 (Nigel French); Gareth Boden pp. **4–5**, **6**, **7**, **8**, **10–11**, **22–23**; Image State p. **19** (David Lissy); Tudor Photography pp. **13** bottom, **14–15**.

Cover photograph reproduced with permission of Angela Hampton.

The publishers would like to thank Annie Davy for her assistance in the preparation of this book.

Every effort has been made to contact copyright holders of any material reproduced in this book. Any omissions will be rectified in subsequent printings if notice is given to the publishers.

# Contents

# Safety on the road

Do you like going out for a walk?

To stay safe there are a few things you need to watch out for.

# Stay on the pavement

Cars **zoom** along the road very **fast**.

Where should you walk?

On the pavement.

7

# Hold hands

The best way to stay safe is to always hold hands with a grown-up, like your mum and dad or your teacher.

STAY
SAFE

BOing

Darren has dropped his ball.

Should he run after it?

NO!

# Cross safely

STOP CHILDREN

crossing patrol assistant

Look both ways!

# Say NO to strangers

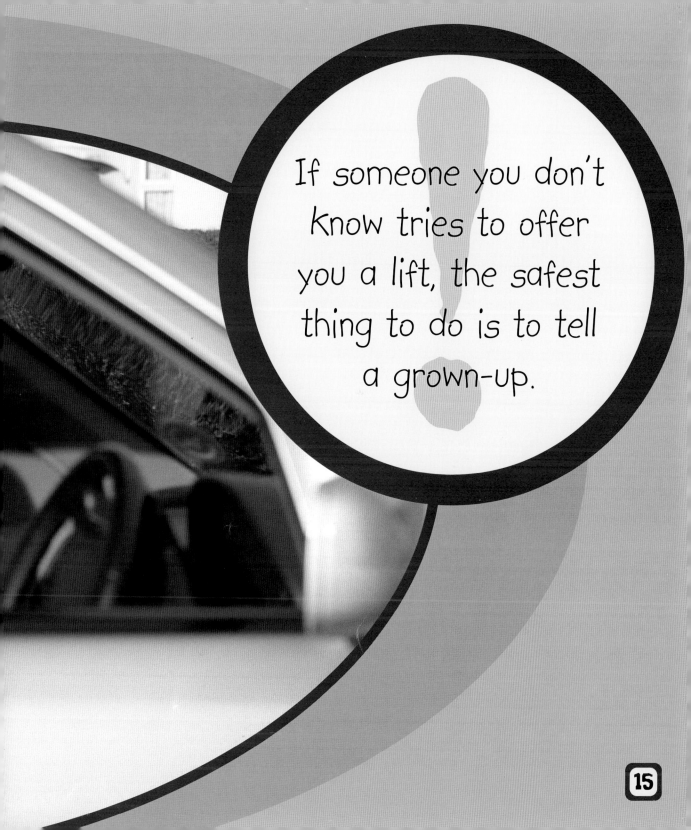

If someone you don't know tries to offer you a lift, the safest thing to do is to tell a grown-up.

# Wear reflective clothing

Cars can see light colours best in the **dark**.

# Protect yourself

Matthew is wearing a helmet to keep him safe on his bike.

# The police

Who is around to make sure that you stay safe?

The police

# Follow the rules

Follow these rules
Make a start
You'll stay safe
And you'll be smart!

23

# Index

The end

## Notes for adults

*Stay Safe!* supports young children's knowledge and understanding of the world around them. The four books will help children to connect safely with the ever-expanding world in which they find themselves. The following Early Learning Goals are relevant to this series:
• move with confidence, imagination and in safety
• move with control and co-ordination
• show awareness of space, of themselves and of others
• use a range of small and large equipment
• handle tools, objects, construction and malleable materials safely and with increasing control
• understand what is right, what is wrong, and why
• dress and undress independently and manage their own personal hygiene.

The *Stay Safe!* series will help children to think more about the potential dangers they will face as they grow up. Discussion can be focused on what makes an activity safe or unsafe allowing the children to learn how to protect themselves from harm. The books can be used to help children understand how their own behaviour can make a difference to their safety.

**On the road** will help children extend their vocabulary, as they will hear new words such as *pavement, subway, pelican crossing, assistant, strangers, reflective, protect, helmet* and *police*.

**Follow-up activities**
• Cut strips of material: dark, light and reflective. In a darkened room, shine a light on to the different materials and ask which one shows up more in the light. Discuss how this could be used to help the children stay safe on the road.
• Draw a layout of a road system on a large sheet of paper or card including crossing points and pavements. Ask how to get from one point to another safely.